■SCHOLASTIC

News

Nonfiction Readers

Wright Brothers

by
Lisa Wade McCormick

Children's Press®
A Division of Scholastic Inc.
New York Toronto London Auckland Sydney
Mexico City New Delhi Hong Kong
Danbury, Connecticut

These content vocabulary word builders
are for grades 1-2.

Consultant:
Dr. Gary Bradshaw
Mississippi State University

Photo Credits:

Photographs © 2005: Air Force Historical Research Agency, Maxwell Air Force Base: 21 bottom left; AP/Wide World Photos: 2 (Thierry Boccon-Gibod), 21 bottom right (Ryan Soderlin/Salina Journal); Brown Brothers: 13; Corbis Images: 20 top (Bettmann), 23 top right (Benjamin Rondel), 21 top (Schenectady Museum/Hall of Electrical History Foundation), back cover (Georges Scott/Bettmann), 23 bottom left (Jeff Vinick/Reuters), 4 bottom right, 5 bottom left, 9, 17; Getty Images: 23 top left; Holiday Film Corp.: cover background, 5 top left, 19; Library of Congress: 4 bottom left, 11, 16; NASA: 23 bottom right; Smithsonian Institution, Washington, DC: cover foreground, 1, 5 bottom right, 7; Superstock, Inc.: 20 bottom; Wright State University/Special Collections and Archives: 4 top, 5 top right, 14, 15.

Book Design: Simonsays Design!

Library of Congress Cataloging-in-Publication Data

McCormick, Lisa Wade, 1961-
    Wright brothers / by Lisa Wade McCormick.
        p. cm. — (Scholastic news nonfiction readers)
    Includes bibliographical references and index.
    ISBN 0-516-24937-1 (lib. bdg.)   0-516-24786-7 (pbk.)
    1. Wright, Wilbur, 1867-1912—Juvenile literature. 2. Wright, Orville,
        1871-1948—Juvenile literature. 3. Aeronautics—United States—
        Biography—Juvenile literature. 4. Aeronautics—United States—
        History—Juvenile literature. I. Title. II. Series.
    TL540.W7M37943 2005
    629.13'0092'273—dc22
                                                            2005003290

1 2 3 4 5 6 7 8 9 10 R 14 13 12 11 10 09 08 07 06 05

CONTENTS

WORD HUNT

Look for these words as you read. They will be in **bold**.

engine
(**en**-juhn)

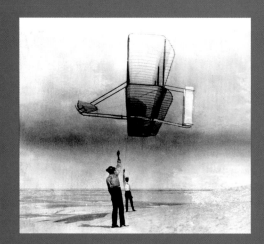

glider
(**glye**-dur)

machine
(muh-**sheen**)

4

flight
(flite)

Flyer
(**fli**-uhr)

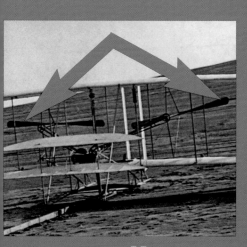

propellers
(pruh-**pel**-urs)

Wright Brothers
(rite **bruh**-thurz)

Meet The Wright brothers!

Wilbur and Orville Wright were brothers.

In the late 1800s, most people traveled on trains, boats, or bicycles.

Wilbur and Orville wanted to fly.

Orville

Wilbur

7

Wilbur and Orville knew that other people had tried to build flying **machines**.

Many people laughed at those machines.

Wilbur and Orville studied them.

Otto Lilienthal was an inventor.
He tried to build flying machines, too.

Wilbur and Orville liked to make things.

They built toys, bicycles, and many other gadgets.

In 1899, the **Wright brothers** built their first plane.

It was a **glider**.

Orville and Wilbur tested their glider before flying it.

The glider had wings made from wood and cloth.

The wings moved from side to side.

The wind helped it to fly.

This is one of the brothers flying the glider.

Wilbur and Orville put an **engine** on their plane.

They added **propeller** push the plane forward.

This plane was called the *Flyer*.

propellers

engine

An engine, propellers, and the wind helped the *Flyer* to fly.

On December 17, 1903
Orville flew the first plane
with an engine.

He took off from Kitty
Hawk, North Carolina.

Kitty Hawk

The wind speed at Kitty Hawk would help the *Flyer* to fly.

Orville stayed in the air for 12 seconds.

He flew 120 feet.

That's as long as three school buses!

Five people saw Orville make that **flight**.

He and Wilbur proved that people could fly.

Time To Fly!

1 In 1900, Ferdinand Graf von Zeppelin builds the first airship.

2 In 1927, Charles Lindbergh flies the *Spirit of St. Louis* **across the Atlantic Ocean alone.**

3 In 1932, Amelia Earhart is the first woman to fly across the Atlantic Ocean alone.

5 In 1953, Jacqueline Cochran becomes the first woman to travel at the speed of sound.

6 In 2005, Steve Fossett flies *GlobalFlyer* nonstop around the world. The flight takes 67 hours.

4 In 1942, The Tuskegee Airmen become the first African American men to become military pilots.

YOUR NEW WORDS

engine (**en**-juhn) a machine that makes things go or gives them power

flight (flite) the act of flying

flyer (**fli**-uhr) the names of the first airplane with an engine

glide (**glye**-dur) a flying machine that uses wind for power

machine (muh-**sheen**) something made with moving parts that does a job

propellers (pruh-**pel**-urs) parts of an airplane that spin and push, or pull, the airplane forward

Wright brothers (rite **bruh**-thurz) brothers who flew the first airplane with an engine

What Else Can Fly?

A Blackbird!

A Concorde!

A jumbo jet!

The space shuttle!

INDEX

FIND OUT MORE
Book:
The Wright Brothers by Ginger Wadsworth
(Lerner Publication Company, 2003)

Website:
Smithsonian National Air and Space Museum
www.nasm.si.edu/wrightbrothers

MEET THE AUTHOR

Lisa Wade McCormick is an award-winning journalist.
She's won two Emmys for investigative reporting. Lisa and
her husband, Dave, have two children—Wade and Madison.
They live in Kansas City, Missouri, and like to fly in airplanes,
just like the Wright Brothers.